Commerce

and

Tourism Management

:: Author ::

Nilamben H. Sondarva

(M.COM.,B.ed., SLET)

PUBLISHED BY

The New ERa International Publishing House
HQ. At & Po. Chaveli., Ta- Chansma,
Dist- Patan, North Gujarat, India, Asia.
www.iphouseindia.com

First Publication: 28TH January, 2015

Copyright: Author
(c) Nilamben H. Sondarva

ISBN:- 978-15-08712-18-3

Price: Rs.750/- INDIA
$ 15 OUTSIDE INDIA

PUBLISHED BY

The New ERa International Publishing House
HQ. At & Po. Chaveli., Ta- Chansma,
Dist- Patan, North Gujarat, India, Asia.
www.iphouseindia.com

Contents

CHAPTER - 1
HISTORY OF TOURISM.

Definition of Tourism.

In 1936, the League of Nations defined a foreign tourist as "someone traveling abroad for at least twenty-four hours". Its successor, the United Nations, amended this definition in 1945, by including a maximum stay of six months. In 1941, Hunziker and Krapf defined tourism as "the sum of the phenomena and relationships arising from the travel and stay of non-residents, insofar as they do not lead topermanent residence and are not connected with any earning activity." In 1976, the Tourism Society of England's definition was: "Tourism is the temporary, short-term movement of people to destinations outside the places where they normally live and work and their activities during the stay at each destination. It includes movements for all purposes." In 1981, the International Association of Scientific Experts in Tourism defined tourism in terms of particular activities chosen and undertaken outside the home.

In 1994, the United Nations identified three forms of tourism in its Recommendations on Tourism Statistics. The terms tourism and travel are sometimes used interchangeably. In this context, travel has a similar definition to tourism, but implies a more purposeful journey. The terms tourism and tourist are sometimes used pejoratively, to imply a shallow interest in the cultures or locations visited.

By contrast, traveler is often used as a sign of distinction. The sociology of tourism has studied the cultural values underpinning these distinctions and their implications for class relations.

Significance of tourism

Tourism is an important, even vital, source of income for many countries. Its importance was recognized in the Manila Declaration on World Tourism of 1980 as "an activity essential to the life of nations because of its direct effects on the social, cultural, educational, and economic sectors of national societies and on their international relations."

Tourism brings in large amounts of income into a local economy in the form of payment for goods and services needed by tourists, accounting for 30% of the world's trade of services, and 6% of overall exports of goods and services. It also creates opportunities for employment in the service sector of the economy associated with tourism.

The service industries which benefit from tourism include transportation services, such as airlines, cruise ships, and taxicabs; hospitality services, such as accommodations, including hotels and resorts; and entertainment venues, such as amusement parks, casinos, shopping malls, music venues, and theatres. This is in addition to goods bought by tourists, including souvenirs, clothing and other supplies.

Tourism could be categorized as:

Domestic Tourism

Domestic tourism involves trips made by local residents within their own countries. Example: An American, who lives in New York, takes a business trip to Los Angeles.

International Tourism

International Tourism involves trips between 2 countries. To a certain country, visits by residents of that country to another country is her outbound tourism , visits to that country by residents of another country is her inbound tourism.

Example: Trips between Hong Kong and Japan. Hong Kong as the point of origin/point of Destination:

➢ Visits made by Hong Kong residents to Japan are Hong Kong's outbound tourism

➢ Visits made by Japanese to Hong Kong are Hong Kong's inbound tourism

Tourism is travel for recreation, leisure, religious, family or business purposes, usually for a limited duration. Tourism is commonly associated with international travel, but may also refer to travel to another place within the same country. he World Tourism Organization defines tourists as people "traveling to and staying in places outside their usual environment for not more than one consecutive year for leisure, business and other purposes".

Tourism has become a popular global leisure activity. ourism can be domestic or international, and international tourism has both incoming and outgoing implications on a country's balance of payments. Today, tourism is a major source of income for many countries, and affects the economy of both the source and host countries, in some cases being of vital importance.

Introduction

Tourism is the act of travel for predominantly recreational or leisure purposes, and also refers to the provision of services in support of this act. According to the World Tourism Organization, tourists are people who "travel to and stay in places outside their usual environment for not more than one consecutive year for leisure, business and other purposes not related to the exercise of an activity remunerated from within the place visited".

Tourism, however long its incident duration, has become an extremely popular, global activity. In 2004, there were over 763 million international tourist arrivals.

As a service industry, tourism has numerous tangible and intangible elements. Major tangible elements include transportation, accommodation, and other components of a hospitality industry. Major intangible elements relate to the purpose or motivation for becoming a tourist, such as rest, relaxation, the opportunity to meet new people and experience other cultures, or simply to do something different and have an adventure.

Tourism is vital for many countries, due to the income generated by the consumption of goods and services by tourists, the taxes levied on businesses in the tourism industry, and the opportunity for employment and economic advancement by working in the industry.

For these reasons NGOs and government agencies may sometimes promote a specific region as a tourist destination, and support the development of a tourism industry in that area.

The contemporary phenomenon of mass tourism may sometimes result in overdevelopment, however alternative forms of tourism such as ecotourism seek to avoid such outcomes by pursuing tourism in a sustainable way. The terms tourism and travel are sometimes used interchangeably. In this context travel has a similar definition to tourism, but implies a more purposeful journey. The terms tourism and tourist are sometimes used pejoratively to imply a shallow interest in the cultures or locations visited by tourists. Tourism embraces nearly all aspects of our society.

Apart from its importance to economic changes, human socio-cultural activities and environmental development, tourism is related to other academic subjects such as geography, economics, history, languages, psychology, marketing, business and law, etc. Therefore, it is necessary to integrate a number of subjects to study tourism. For example, subjects such as history and geography help us understand more about the development of the historical and geographical resources of a tourist destination. Besides, subjects like marketing and business help us understand the promotion and marketing of tourism products. Tourism is a complex field of study because it includes a variety of disciplines which are either directly or indirectly related to the understanding of tourism. The study of information technology enhances our understanding of the importance of the global distribution system and its effect on tourism business.

The study of religion and culture provides information on the cultural resources of a destination and opportunities to develop it as a cultural destination. Tourism is so vast, so complex, and so multifaceted that there is a wide range of subjects related to tourism.

Integrated Model of Tourism and its 3 Major Components

The vast majority of business organizations such as travel agents, meeting planners, and other service providers including accommodation, transportation, attractions and entertainment are classified as travel and tourism related business. In practice, these organizations are closely linked in the provision of services to the travellers. Tourism is so vast, so complex, and somultifaceted that the practitioners need to obtain a wide range of knowledge related to tourism

Travellers

Travellers are at the centre of the model where all tourism activities are focused. Radiating from the centre are three large bands containing several interdependent groups of tourism participants and organizations.

Tourism Promoters

Tourism promoters are in the first layer, in close contact with the travellers. Organizations in this layer include tourism boards, direct marketing companies, meeting planners, travel agents and tour operators. The tourism boards and direct marketing companies provide information and marketing services to travelers whereas travel agencies, tour operators and meeting planners provide services such as making travel arrangements and giving professional advice on tourism related matters.

All these organizations usually deal directly with individual travellers.

Tourism Service Suppliers

Tourism service suppliers, such as airline companies, bus operators, railway corporations, cruise ship operators, hotels and car rental companies, etc. usually provide services to travellers independently. The service suppliers may also collaborate to provide tour packages for travellers by combining the various services such as accommodation, air transportation, theme park entrance ticket, etc.

External Environment

All of the participants, either individually or as a group, are constantly responding to a variety of societal/cultural, political, environmental, economic and technological forces. It is the interaction of these forces that determine how closely the individuals and organizations work together. Societal/Cultural forces such as the local skill and know how, the indigenous cultures of the destination and the attitude of local people towards the tourists would have a significant impact on the tourist experience in a destination. One example of encouraging the local community to take part in tourism is the "Be a Good Host" campaign launched by the Hong Kong Tourism Board.

It "word-of-mouth" aims at enhancing the tourist experience which helps to promote Hong Kong through Political forces such as government support on infrastructure, its policy on tourism planning, the diplomatic relations between tourist generating countries and tourist destination countries, etc. determines the environment of tourism development.

For example, because of political instability in the Middle East, tourism development in the region and the attractiveness of these countries to tourists has been adversely affected. Environmental forces such as the problems of congestion, pollution, hygienic conditions, loss of green belts caused by excessive urbanization and development of tourism may destroy the pleasant ambiance of the destination which visitors look for. For example, Hong Kong's air pollution problem as a factor discourages tourists to come to Hong Kong.

Economic forces such as the disposable income of tourist and the affordability of a destination affect the desire to travel. For example, in Hong Kong, due to the economic crisis I 1997, the number of visitor arrivals in particular from Asia recorded a negative growth in 1998. (Statistical Review, Hong Kong Tourism Board, 1999). In the recent 2008 global financial crisis, Hong Kong Tourism Board showed that visitor arrivals in November was 1.1% less than in November 2007. 4Technological forces such as the popularity of using the Internet for searching information, reservation or purchasing of tourism products affect the tourists' buying behaviour.

World tourism statistics and ranking.

International tourist arrivals reached 1.035 billion in 2012, up from over 983 million in 2011, and 940 million in 2010. In 2011 and 2012, international travel demandcontinued to recover from the losses resulting from the late-2000s recession, where tourism suffered a strong slowdown from the second half of 2008 through the end of 2009. After a 5% increase in the first half of 2008, growth in international tourist arrivals moved into negative territory in the second half of 2008, and ended up only 2% for the year, compared to a 7% increase in 2007. The negative trend intensified during 2009, exacerbated in some countries due to the outbreak of the H1N1 influenza virus, resulting in a worldwide decline of 4.2% in 2009 to 880 million international tourists arrivals, and a 5.7% decline in international tourism receipts.

World's top 10 tourism destinations
World Tourism rankings

The World Tourism Organization reports the following ten countries as the most visited in terms of the number of international travellers in 2013.

Rank	Country	UNWTO Region[21]	International tourist arrivals (2013)[22]	International tourist arrivals (2012)[22]	Change (2012 to 2013) (%)	Change (2011 to 2012) (%)
1	France	Europe	84.7 million	83.0 million	▲ 2.0	▲ 1.8
2	United States	North America	69.8 million	66.7 million	▲ 4.7	▲ 6.3
3	Spain	Europe	60.7 million	57.5 million	▲ 5.6	▲ 2.3
4	China	Asia	55.7 million	57.7 million	▼ 3.5	▲ 0.3
5	Italy	Europe	47.7 million	46.4 million	▲ 2.9	▲ 0.5
6	Turkey	Europe	37.8 million	35.7 million	▲ 5.9	▲ 3.0
7	Germany	Europe	31.5 million	30.4 million	▲ 3.7	▲ 7.3
8	United Kingdom	Europe	31.2 million	29.3 million	▲ 6.4	▼ 0.1
9	Russia	Europe	28.4 million	25.7 million	▲ 10.2	▲ 13.5
10	Thailand	Asia	26.5 million	22.4 million	▲ 18.8	▲ 16.2

The traditional way of distributing tourism products through intermediaries, such as travel agents, tour wholesalers is facing a great challenge. Now that travellers can deal directly with the suppliers, such as airlines, hotels, operators of attractions to purchase tourism products, they can almost by-pass travel agents.

History of Tourism

Roman Empire Period

During the Roman Empire period (from about 27 BC to AD 476), travel developed for military, trade and political reasons, as well as for communication of messages from the central government to its distant territories. Travel was also necessary for the artisans and architects "imported" to design and construct the great palaces and tombs. In ancient Greece, people traveled to Olympic Games. Both the participants and spectators required accommodations and food services. Wealthy Romans, in ancient times, traveled to seaside resorts in Greece and Egypt for sightseeing purpose.

Middle Age Period

During the Middle Age (from about AD 500 to 1400), there was a growth of travel for religious reasons. It had become an organized phenomenon for pilgrims to visit their "holy land", such as Muslims to Mecca, and Christians to Jerusalem and Rome.

16th Century

In the 16th century, the growth in England's trade and commerce led to the rise of a new type of tourists - those traveled to broaden their own experience and knowledge.

17th Century

In the 17th century, the sons and daughters of the British aristocracy traveled throughout Europe (such as Italy, Germany and France) for periods of time, usually 2 or 3 years, to improve their knowledge. This was known as the Grand Tour, which became a necessary part of the training of future administrators and political leaders.

Industrial Revolution Period

The Industrial Revolution (from about AD 1750 to 1850) in Europe created the base for mass tourism. This period turned most people away from basic agriculture into the town / factory and urban way of life. As a result, there was a rapid growth of the wealth and education level of the middle class, as well as an increase of leisure time and a demand for holiday tourism activities.

At that time, travel for health became important when the rich and fashionable Europeans began to visit the spa towns (such as Bath in England and Baden - Baden in Germany) and seaside resorts in England (such as Scarborough, Margate and Brighton).

19th to 20th Centuries

In the 19th and 20th centuries, the social and technological changes have had an immense impact on tourism. Great advances in science and technology made possible the invention of rapid, safe and relatively cheap forms of transport.

The railways were invented in the 19th century and the passenger aircraft in the 20th century. World War II (AD 1939-1945) was also the impetus for dramatic improvements in communication and air transportation, which made travel much easier today than in earlier times.

1980s

The 1980s were called the boom years. Business and leisure travel expanded very rapidly. The baby-boomers were coming of age and had the money to spend. These travellers were looking for a variety of travel products from exciting vacation options such as adventure travel, ecotourism and luxurious travel. There was not only a significant expansion in the travel market but also in tourist destinations. The fall of the Berlin Wall in Germany in 1989 signified the doom of communism in Europe. Countries such as Russia and the Czech Republic became new tourist destinations both for vacation and business travellers.

1990s

The Aviation Industry was facing high operational costs, including wage, oil prices, handling fee of Central Reservation System (CRS), landing charge of the air crafts and advertising fee etc. During this decade, CRS also marched towards more sophisticated technology. It became possible for agents to book a huge inventory of travel products, such as hotels, car rentals, cruises, rail passes, and theatre tickets from the CRS.

The introduction of "ticketless traveling" (electronic ticket) brings benefits to the airlines by cutting the amount of paperwork and cost of tickets. At the same time, passengers do not have to worry about carrying or losing tickets. Although, electronic ticketing does not bypass the travel agents as intermediaries, it makes it easier for the airline to deal directly with consumers. The advance in technology also allows the airlines and other travel suppliers to sell directly to travellers through the Internet and interactive kiosks at airports.

The kiosks at the airport usually sell hotel accommodation, transfer tickets such as bus tickets between airport and downtown areas and coach tickets from one city to another. Travellers can now log on to the Internet easily reach for travel information, book a simple ticket or hotel room through their personal computer at home. There are thousands of new destinations, tour products and discounted airfares for travellers to choose from.

CHAPTER – 2
OBJECTIVES AND TYPES OF TOURISM

We have discussed in the previous units in detail, that tourism industry is one of the major segments of the Indian economy. It is a major contributor to foreign exchange earnings provides employment to millions directly and indirectly and acts as a vehicle for infrastructure development. Recognising the importance of the tourism industry, the Government of India has taken many policy measures such as Tourism Policy 1982, Tourism Plan of Action 1992 and Tourism Policy 1997. Through these policies, the government called for effective coordination of public and private participation to achieve synergy in the development of tourism.

These plans identified new forms of tourism products for taking advantage of the emerging markets. Business tourism, health tourism, rural tourism, pilgrim tourism, adventure tourism, and sustainable tourism are some of the new products devised for changing demand. Let us study these emerging dimensions in the tourism sector.

OBJECTIVES

After studying this unit you will be able to achieve following objectives:

➢ Understand emerging trends in tourism.

➢ Learn about new products and old traditional tourism products.

➢ Know the importance of sustainable tourism development.

➢ Understand the concept of nature tourism.

➢ Develop environmental consciousness.

➢ Develop skills to locate important tourist destinations on the map.

➢ Know that tourism can be an instrumental for developing secularism

➢ National integration and universal brotherhood.

EMERGING DIMENSIONS

Tourism will expand greatly in future mainly due to the revolution that is taking place on both the demand and supply side.

The changing population structure, improvement in living standard, more disposable income, fewer working hours and long leisure time, better educated people, ageing population and more curious youth in developing the countries, all will fuel the tourism industry growth. The arrival of a large number of customers, better educated and more sophisticated, will compel the tourist industry to launch new products and brands and re-invents traditional markets. The established traditional destinations founded on sun-sea-sand products will have to re-engineer their products.

They must diversify and improve the criteria for destinations and qualities of their traditional offers. Alongside beach tourism, the tourism sector will register a steady development of new products based on natural rural business, leisure and art and culture.

Thus the study of new markets and emerging markets and necessity of diversified products are the basis of our strategy, which can enhance and sustain, existing and capture new markets. Let us discuss some of the new tourism products.

Business tourism

Business tourism or business travel is a more limited and focused subset of regular tourism. During business tourism (traveling), individuals are still working and being paid, but are doing so away from both their workplace and home. Some definitions of tourism tend to exclude business travel. However, the World Tourism Organization (WTO) defines tourists as people "traveling to and staying in places outside their usual environment for not more than one consecutive year for leisure, business and other purposes". Primary business tourism activities include meetings, and attending conferences and exhibitions.

Despite the term business in business tourism, when individuals from government or non-profit organizations engage in similar activities, this is still categorized as business tourism (travel).

Significance

Historically, business tourism, is in the form of traveling to, spending money and staying abroad, away for some time, has a history as long as that of international trade. In late 20th century, business tourism is seen as a major industry. According to the 1998 data from the British Tourist Authority and National

Tourist Boards, business tourism accounted for about 14% of all trips to or within UK, and 15% of the tourist market within UK.

A 2005 estimate suggested that those numbers for UK may be closer to 30% cited a WTO estimated that business tourism accounts for 30% of international tourism, through its importance varies significantly between different countries.

Characteristics

Compared to regular tourism, business ones involves a smaller section of the population, with different motivations, and additional freedom-of-choice limiting constrains imposed through the business aspects. Destinations of business tourism are much more likely to be areas significantly developed for business purposes (cities, industrial regions, etc.). An average business tourist is more wealthy than an average leisure tourist, and is expected to spend more money.

Business tourism can be divided into primary and secondary activities. Primary one are business (work) related, and included activities such as consultations, inspections, and attending meetings. Secondary ones are related to tourism (leisure) and include activities such as dining out, recreation, shopping, sightseeing, meeting others for leisure activities, and so on. While the primary ones are seen as more important, the secondary ones are nonetheless often described as "substantial".

Business tourism can involve individual and small group travel, and destinations can include small to larger meetings, including conventions   and   conferences, trade   fairs, andexhibitions. In the United States, about half of business tourism involves attending a large meeting of such kind.Most tourist facilities such as airports, restaurants and hotels are shared between leisure and business tourists, through a seasonal difference is often apparent (for example, business tourism may use those facilities during times less attractive for leisure tourists, such as when the weather conditions are less attractive). Business tourism can be divided into:

➢ traditional business traveling, or meetings - intended for face-to-face meetings with business partners in different locations

➢ incentive trips - a job perk, aimed at motivating employees (for example, approximately a third of UK companies use this strategy to motivate workers

➢ conference and exhibition traveling - intended for attending large scale meetings. In an estimated number of 14,000 conferences worldwide (for 1994), primary destinations are Paris, London, Madrid, Geneva, Brussels, Washington, New York, Sydney and Singapore

Cultural tourism

Cultural tourism (or culture tourism) is the subset of tourism concerned with a country or region's culture, specifically the lifestyle of the people in those geographical areas, the history of those people, their art, architecture, religion(s), and other elements that helped shape their way of life. Cultural tourism includes tourism in urban areas, particularly historic or large cities and their cultural facilities such as<u>museums</u> and <u>theatres</u>.

It can also include tourism in rural areas showcasing the traditions of indigenous cultural communities (i.e. festivals, rituals), and their values and lifestyle, as well as niches like <u>industrial tourism</u> and creative tourism. It is generally agreed that cultural tourists spend substantially more than standard tourists do. This form of tourism is also becoming generally more popular throughout the world, and a recent OECD report has highlighted the role that cultural tourism can play in regional development in different world regions. Cultural tourism has been defined as 'the movement of persons to cultural attractions away from their normal place of residence, with the intention to gather new information and experiences to satisfy their cultural needs'. These cultural needs can include the solidification of one's own cultural identity, by observing the exotic "other".

Key Principles
Destination Planning

As the issue of <u>globalization</u> takes place in this modern time, the challenge of preserving the few remaining cultural community around the world is becoming hard. In a tribal based community, reaching <u>economic</u> advancement with minimal negative impacts is an essential objective to any destination planner. Since they are using the culture of the region as the main attraction, sustainable destination development of the area is vital for them to prevent the negative impacts (i.e. destroying the authentic identity of the tribal community) due to tourism.

Management Issues

Certainly, the principle of "one size fits all" doesn't apply to destination planning. The needs, expectations, and anticipated benefits from tourism vary greatly from one destination to another. This is clearly exemplified as local communities living in regions with tourism potential (destinations) develop a vision for what kind of tourism they want to facilitate, depending on issues and concerns they want to be settled or satisfied.

It is important that the destination planner takes into account the diverse definition of <u>culture</u> as the term is subjective. Satisfying tourists' interests such as landscapes, seascapes, art, nature, traditions, ways of life and other products associated to them -which may be categorized cultural in the broadest sense of the word, is a prime consideration as it marks the initial phase of the development of a cultural destination.

The quality of service and destination, which doesn't solely depend on the cultural heritage but more importantly to the cultural environment, can further be developed by setting controls and policies which shall govern the community and its stakeholders. It is therefore safe to say that the planner should be on the ball with the varying meaning of culture itself as this fuels the formulation of development policies that shall entail efficient planning and monitored growth (e.g. strict policy on the protection and preservation of the community).

Local community, tourists, the destination and sustainable tourism

While satisfying tourists' interests and demands may be a top priority, it is also imperative to ruminate the subsystems of the destination's (residents). Development pressures should be anticipated and set to their minimum level so as to conserve the area's resources and prevent a saturation of the destination as to not abuse the product and the residents correspondingly.

The plan should incorporate the locals to its gain by training and employing them and in the process encourage them to participate to the travel business. Travellers should be not only aware about the destination but also concern on how to help it sustain its character while broadening their travelling experience.

Research on Tourism

International Tourism changes the world. The Centre for Tourism and Cultural Change (CTCC) is leading internationally in approaching Tourism for critical research relating to the relationships between tourism, tourists and culture.

One type of cultural tourism destination is living cultural areas. Visiting any culture other than one's own such as traveling to a foreign country. Other destinations include historical sites, modern urban districts, "ethnic pockets" of town, fairs/festivals, theme parks, and natural ecosystems. It has been shown that cultural attractions and events are particularly strong magnets for tourism.The term cultural tourism is used for journeys that include visits to cultural resources, regardless of whether it is tangible or intangible cultural resources, and regardless of the primary motivation. In order to understand properly the concept of cultural tourism, it is necessary to know the definitions of a number terms such as, for example, culture, tourism, cultural economy, cultural and tourism potentials, cultural and tourist offer, and others.

TYPES OF TOURISM
HEALTH TOURISM

India is promoting the high-tech healing provided by its private health care sector as a tourist attraction. This budding trade in medical tourism, selling foreigners the idea of travelling to India for world-class medical treatment at lowest cost, has really got attention in the overseas market. The Indian system of medicine, which incorporates ayurveda, yoga, sidha, unani, naturopathy and other traditional healing treatments, is very unique and exotic.

This medical expertise coupled with allopathic and other modern methods become our new focus segment to project India as a Global Healing Destination. If we believe the report published by McKenzie Consultants and Confederation of Indian Industries (CII), the response is quite positive and it could be generating revenue approximately Rs.100b by the year 2012. Our medical tourism provides low cost treatment. Perhaps you will wonder that the cost of same treatment in the US is ten times more than that in India. Many state governments like Kerala, Andhra Pradesh, Uttranchal, and Karnataka have been showcasing their medical tourism segment in certain focused market like the Gulf and African regions.

Indian private sector hospitals have undertaken massive investment in the area of health. These super-specialty hospitals employ efficient and expert doctors and other paramedical staffs with modern facilities. The experienced doctors, dedicated service minded experts have made available their services for giving alternative system of medicines and treatments.

Health camps, lecture training classes are also arranged for general awareness. Yogasana has become popular and widespread and many public and private and other organisations conduct Yoga classes. Ayurveda, naturopathy and nature treatments are popular around the world.

Total Health: A New Mantra Ayurveda

India has a rich heritage in the areas of traditional and natural medicines. The earliest mention of Indian medical practices can be found in the Vedas and Samhitas of Charaka, Bhela and Shusruta.

A systematic and scientific approach was adopted by the sages of the time leading to the development of a system that is relevant even today. India is the land of Ayurveda. It believes in removing the cause of illness and not just curing the disease itself. It is based on herbals and herbal components without having side effects. Ayurveda considers that the base of life lies in the five primary elements; ether (space), air, fire, water and earth. And the individual is made up of a unique proportion of the five elements in unique combinations to form three doshas (vata, pita and kapha). When any of these doshas become accute, a person falls ill.

Ayurveda recommends a special life style and nutritional guidelines supplemented with herbal medicines. If toxins are abundant, then a cleaning process known as Panchkarma is recommended to eliminate those unwanted toxins and revitalize both mind and body. Ayurveda offers treatments for ailments such as arthritis, paralysis, obesity, sinusitis, migraine, premature aging and general health care.

Kerala is a world tourist destination and part of the reasons lies with the well- known stress-releasing therapies of famed Ayurvedic research centers. The climate along with the blessing of nature has turned Kerala into the ideal place for ayurvedic, curative and rejuvenating treatments.

Yoga

If Ayurveda is the science of body, yoga is the science of the mind. Practiced together they can go a long way in making an individual fit. The word yoga means to join together. The ultimate aim of yoga is to unite the human soul with the universal spirit. Yoga was developed 5000 years ago and the base of yoga is described in the Yoga Sutra of Patanjali. This describes eight stages of yoga.

These are Yam (universal moral commands), Niyam (self purification), Asana (posture), Pranayama (breathing control), Prathyahara (withdrawal of mind from external objects), Dharana (concentration), Dhyana (meditation), and Samadhi (state of superconsciousness). To get the benefits of yoga, one has to practice Asana, Pranayama and Yoganidra.

Spas

Most of the other parts of the world have their own therapies and treatment that are no doubt effective in restoring wellness and beauty. New kinds of health tours that are gaining popularity in India are spa tours. Spas offer the unique advantages of taking the best from the west and the east combining them with the indigenous system and offering best of the two worlds.

In hydropathy, Swedish massages work with the Javanese Mandy, lulur, aromatherapy, reflexology and traditional ayurveda procedures to help keep the tourist healthy and enhance beauty. Combining these therapies with meditation, yoga and pranayama make the spa experience in India a new destination for medical tourism.

The spas are very useful for controlling blood pressure, insomnia, cure tension, depression, paralysis and number of other deadly diseases. Ananda Resort in Rishikesh, Angsana Resort, Golden Palm Spa and Ayurgram in Bangalore offer ayurveda, naturopathy, yoga and meditation packages. (Gaur Kanchilal)

Allopathy

India has made rapid strides in advanced health care systems, which provides world-class allopathic treatment. This has become possible because of the emergence of the private sector in a big way in this field. More and more foreign tourists are realizing that India is an ideal place for stopover treatment. Indian Multi-specialty hospitals are providing worldclass treatment at an amazingly economical cost as compared to the west. Quality services and low price factor primarily go in favour of India. The cardio care, bone marrow transplantation, dialysis, kidney transplant, neuron–surgery, joint replacement surgery, urology, osteoporosis and numerous diseases are treated at Indian hospitals with full professional expertise.

Apollo hospital group, Escorts in Delhi, Jason Hospital, Global Hospital, and Max Health Care are catering to medical care for international patients in the areas of diagnostic, disease management, preventive health care and incisive surgeries.

The tourism department has devised websites in order to provide information. Many Ayurveda health resorts that are owned and rum by traditional Ayurveda Institutes have come up. Ayurgram is a novel concept that not only offers heritage accommodation but also offers a whole range of Ayurvedic treatments and rejuvenating packages. Similarly hotels have also included these types of packages in their holidays. Some of the tour operators have worked out all-inclusive medical treatment package that include treatment, accommodation, food, airport transfers, post operation recuperative holidays, along with a host of other facilities.

SPIRITUAL TOURISM

Globally people are increasingly mentally disturbed and looking for solace in spiritual reading, meditation and moments of divine ecstasy. Our country has been known as the seat of spiritualism and India's cosmopolitan nature is best reflected in its pilgrim centres. Religion is the life-blood for followers of major religion and sects. Hinduism, Islam, Buddhism, Jainism, Zoroastrianism and Christianity have lived here for centuries. The visible outpouring of religious fervor is witnessed in the architecturally lavish temples, mosques, monasteries and Churches spreads across the length and breadth of the country. India is not only known as a place rich in its culture with varied attractions but also for many places of worship, present itself as embodiments of compassion where one get peace of mind. Thus India has been respected as a destination for spiritual tourism for domestic and international tourists. Spiritual tourism is also termed as religious heritage tourism. It includes all the religions mentioned above; religious places associated with, emotional attachment to these centers and infrastructure facilities for the tourists. This can also be referred to as pilgrimage tourism, as clients are not looking for luxury but arduous journeys to meet the divine goal or simple life.

The essence of spiritual tourism is inner feeling through love. Love should not be rationed on the basis of caste, creed and economic status or intellectual attainment of the recipient. Religions come into existence for the purpose of regulating human life; what are common to all of them are the principles of love.

Thus through religious tourism there is a sincere effort to bring better understanding among various communities, nations and thus foster global unity.

Hinduism is one of the oldest religions of India. Over 5000 years of religious history created wonderful temples and survived through ages all over India. The most popular spiritual tours are those that are centered on holy Ganges River. Badrinath, Kedarnath, Haridwar, Gangotri, Yamunotri, Allahabad, Varanasi. Jaganath temple at Puri, Bhubaneshwar, Konark in Orissa, Mata Vaishnodevi of Jammu and Kashmir, are some of the important pilgrim centers in north India. There are many spiritual sites in South India as well which dates back beyond the 10th centaury. Rameshwaram, Mahabalipuram, Madurai Meenakshi temple in Tamilnadu and Tirupati in Andhra Pradesh are some pilgrim centers. Every year millions of tourists, both domestic and international, visit these places.

India is special to Buddhists all over the world and India is the destination for pilgrimage because Buddhism emerged in India. The country is dotted with places that are associated with the life and times of Gutham Buddha; Lumbini-the birthplace of

Buddha, Saranath where Buddha delivered his first sermon, Buddha Gaya where lord Buddha attained enlightenment and Vaishali where he delivered his last sermon and announced his nirvana.

Sikhism also emerged in India. The Golden Temple in Amritsar, the Hemkund Sahib, and Gurunanak Devji Gurudwara at Manikaran, which is also known for its hot water springs with healing properties, the holy city of Patna Sahib and Anandpur Sahib are important for Sikhs. The Jain temples of Dilwara and Mount Abu in Rajasthan, the Gomateswara temple at Karnataka, draw thousands of Jain followers. Even small communities like the Bahais have their own Lotus Temple at Delhi. The Sultanate and Moghul empires built many hist orical monuments andmosques during their reign, all over the country. Red Fort, Fatehapur Sikri, Jama Masjid, TajMahal, Charminar etc., bear testimony to the blend of the Indian and Islam traditions of architecture. The followers of Islam have many mosques and shrines of Sufi Saints, like Moin-Uddin Chisti and Nizamuddin Aulia. For Christians, spiritual tours to Goa among other place like Mumbai and Kolkata are must. Among the most popular sites in Goa is the church of Our Lady of Rosary, the Rachel Seminary, and Church of Bom Jesus. In addition to pilgrim centers there are personalities like the Satya Sai Baba, Osho, Shirdhi and others. This shows that spirituality and religion in India is a serious pursuit. The State Governments concerned, charitable trusts, temple trusts have made elaborate arrangements for accommodation, transport and ritual ceremonies. These organizations are also running hospitals, educational institutes, ashrams, meditation centers which benefit local community. More than 500 religious places have been identified and efforts are being made to develop these centers by Central and State Governments with private participation.

MICE TOURISM

The meetings, incentives, conferences and exhibitions (MICE) industry is extensively and rapidly growing and is largely associated with travel for business purpose. MICE related events include meetings, conferences, conventions, exhibitions and incentive travels. Each of these different subsections of MICE has quite different characteristics although the industry is often referred to as MICE. Increasingly convention bureaus serve the needs of meetings, incentives and exhibitions organizers and service providers supply each of the sectors. Business with Pleasure With the Indian economy opening up and government restrictions loosening, Mumbai, Bangalore, Hyderabad, Chennai, Delhi and Kolkata are assuming importance as major centres of business activity in the country.

The days of red- tape always associated with Indian business activity is a thing of the past and corporate India has moved towards more western standards of professionalism. Since the liberalization of the Indian economy, MICE tourism is becoming a growing segment in India. More and more business people have been coming to India for business purpose and adding business with pleasure in their India tour.

Most of the hotels and tour operators offer special facilities for travelers some even specialized in this field. They offers pick-up at the airport, corporate floor rooms which will feature phones, fax machines, computers, journals. All rooms offer elaborate conferencing facilities at hotels and special conventions centers. Hotels are adept in organizing theme banquets for a product launch, small cocktails etc. The important conference centers are New Delhi, Mumbai, Jaipur, Kovalam, Chennai, Bangalore, Agra, and Goa where popular convention tours offer exciting possibilities. Incentive tourism Incentive travel has emerged as a popular means of rewarding the employees' achievements and contributions, by several business houses especially multinational companies, Insurance Companies, Banks, Pharmaceuticals Firms, etc. Employees are given free tickets or holidays packages to select destinations all paid by company.

These are given as added perks to keep up the interest of the executives who are the high performers of the company. Incentive tours market has become fast growing sector within the tourism industry.

ADVENTURE TOURISM

Youth tourism has been identified as one of the largest segments of global and domestic tourism. The young travellers are primarily experience seekers, collecting, enquiring unique experiences. Adventure and risk have a special role to play in the behaviour and attitudes of young travellers. The growing number of young travellers is being fuelled by a number of factors such as increased participation in higher education, falling level of youth unemployment, increased travel budget through parental contribution, search for an even more exciting and unique experience and cheaper long distance travel.

Youth and adventure tourism appears to have considerable growth potential. The rising income in some major potential source markets such as the Central and Eastern Europe, Asia and Latin America, combined with the lower travel cost, growing student populations around the world particularly in developing countries, has fuelled the demand. India: a heaven for adventure tourism India has been an attraction for travellers from all over the world. Though in the field of international tourism, the segment of adventure tourism in India is getting only a fraction of such traffic.

The trend has been showing an increased movement year after year with the development of facilities and greater awareness about adventure tourism options. Indian tourism offers both international and domestic adventurers a wide choice of adventures.

Water sports, elephant safari, skiing, yachting, hail-skiing, gliding, sailing, tribal tours, orchid tours, scaling the high peaks of Himalayas, trekking to the valley of flowers, riding the waves in rapids, and camel safari in the deserts are breath taking opportunities for nature enthusias. Ladakh, the Garwal hills, the Himachal hills, Darjeeling, Goa, Lakshadweep, Andaman and Nicobar, Jaisalmer and wildlife sanctuaries and reserves are some of the places that offer adventure tourism. Himalayas are the centre of India's main adventure activities as well as outdoor recreational tourism.

Our rivers, backwaters, Indian Ocean, Arabian Sea and deserts are unique attractions for the various branches of adventure. Trekking holds out the greatest potential in terms of numbers. It requires little infrastructure and carries its benefits to remote hills and mountain regions. Many of them are economically poor and backward.

For our own youth it also helps in inculcating a spirit of adventure, respect for nature. Indian Mountaineering Federation, Ministry of Tourism and State Governments are trying to improve trekking facilities and ensure safety and protection of travellers.

The Institute of Mountaineering also organises courses for guides to train them in basic rock climbing safety procedures, environmental knowledge, and flora and fauna conservation. The major trek heads in the Himalayan region include Kashmir valley, Kirshwasser Zanskar, Ladhak, Lahul and Spiti, Champa and Manali, etc, Trekking in the Himalayas is a quite enjoyable. Let us now discuss some important adventure activities:

Mountaineering Expedition

This is the first and foremost activity in the Himalayas. In India, the expeditions are controlled and regulated by Indian Mountaineering Federation, which is the nodal body. Foreign expedition groups have to request the Indian Mountaineering Foundation (IMF) to book the required peak and IMF confirms the peak, by charging the royalty depending upon the number of persons and height of peak. Ministry of Defence, Home Ministry, Ministry of External Affairs are also involved in this process.

River rafting

The Himalayan river's offer River rafting that run through the beautiful terrains, sandy white beaches, boulder studded rapids, river confluences, deep gorges, and some revered temples and towns. White-water sports are popular in Rishikesh, Manali, Zanskar Teesta, Beas, Central Ministry of Tourism has great extremely extended support to import inflatable rafts, canoes, kayaks, and accessories to boost water sports. Lakshadweep and Andaman have been promoted for scuba diving and windsurfing.

NATURE TOURISM

In search of new tourism products, travellers and suppliers are today seeking to reshape the meaning of nature as a tourism attraction. Modern nature based tourism focuses on experiencing flora and fauna in natural settings.

The nature based tourism related to nature, its attractiveness so that the visitors experience it in its natural settings. Eco-tourism takes into account unspoiled natural and socio-cultural attraction. Today the term nature tourism is often used synonymously with eco-tourism. Today nature tourism is the fastest growing segment of the tourism sector. It comprises around 40 - 60% of all international tourism.

Diversity of India is to be seen not only in its people, culture, religions, language and life style, the diversity starts in the land itself. The snowbourd peaks of the Himalayas, tropical rain forests, and hot deserts and breathtaking beautiful coasts. Each diverse geographical region generates a different picture and exploring them provides a unique experience. Now all these are packaged for tourists to provide eco-friendly holidays in India.

Wild life

The diversity of wild life in India is as rich as that of its flora and fauna. The great wealth of Indian wild-life can be imagined with the sight of majestic elephants, the dance of peacocks, the camel strides, the roar of tigers, at unparalleled acts of beauty. Watching birds and animals in their natural habitat is an experience in itself. The vastness of wild life and wilderness is India unparallel in the world. All these account for the immense opportunities for wild life tourism in India. The immense heritage of wild life in India comprises 80 national parks and another whopping 441 wild life sanctuaries including bird sanctuaries.

These reserves and forest areas are spread across the breadth and length right form the foot hills of Himalayan, the Jim Corbet National park to six national parks in Andaman, from Ranthambhor national park in Rajasthan to Hazaribag wild life sanctuary in Bihar. India also boasts of the unique ecosystem at Sunderbans which is a UNESCO world heritage site and home to the largest number of tigers in the world. The Himalayan region is renowned for being the national habitat for a variety of wild life, elephants, snow leopards, deer, panther, wild buffalos, wild ass, one horned rhinoceros, porcupine, snow leopards, etc. The Kaziranga Game Sanctuary is ideal habitat for the rhino that the nature lovers and environmentalists are fascinated by. The great Indian bustard and the black buck of Kerera sanctuary attract a lot of tourists. The Madhav National Park (Shivpuri Park) is another rich habitat for the wild life. The royal animal, tiger happens to be symbol of strength and speed. Amongst the best-known tiger reserves in India is Bandhawgarh in Madhya Pradesh. It is also known as the crown in the wild life heritage of India.

RURAL TOURISM

Rural tourism has been identified as one of the priority areas for development of Indian tourism. Rural tourism experience should be attractive to the tourists and sustainable for the host community.

The Ninth Plan identified basic objectives of rural tourism as: -

➢ Improve the quality of life of rural people
➢ Provide good experience to the tourist
➢ Maintain the quality of environment.

Indian villages have the potential for tourism development. With attractive and unique traditional way of life, rich culture, nature, crafts, folk-lore and livelihood of Indian villages are a promising destination for the tourist. It also provides tourism facilities in terms of accessibility, accommodation, sanitation and security.

Rural tourism can be used as a means to:-
➢ Improve the well being of the rural poor
➢ Empower the rural people
➢ Empower the women
➢ Enhance the rural infrastructure
➢ Participate in decision-making and implementing tourism policies
➢ Interaction with the outside world
➢ Improve the social condition of lower sections of the society.
➢ Protection of culture, heritage, and nature.

To tap the immense opportunities, coordinated actives of all agencies involved in the development are required. A carefully planned and properly implemented development will definitely benefit the community economically and improve the quality of life in the villages. The success of such development depends upon the people's participation at grass root level for the development of tourist facilities and for creating a tourist friendly atmosphere. Development of rural tourism is fast and trade in hotels and restaurants is growing rapidly. Increase in the share of earnings through rural tourism will no doubt; provide an attractive means of livelihood to the poor rural community. It increases the purchasing power at all levels of community and strengthens the rural economy. Development of infrastructure facilities such as rail, electricity, water, health and sanitation will definitely improve the quality of life. Government Initiatives Central Government and State Governments have been encouraging rural handicrafts and fairs and festivals that have direct impact on preservation of heritage and culture of rural India. It also draws tourists from all over the world.

Regional fairs, festivals help the growth of tourism, provide a ready market for the handicrafts, alternative income to the community, and facilitate regional interaction within the country. The state governments have been monitoring closely the ecological relationship, socio cultural impact and conducting feasibility studies before selecting tourist sites.

The state governments also ensure that:
Tourism –

> Does not cause the tension for the host community
> No adverse impact on the resources
> Psychological satisfaction for the tourist.
> The large inflow of tourists would not put a stress on the local system

➤ Local community should not be deprived of basic facilities for the benefits of tourist

➤ The rural tourism does not disrupt the rhythm of community life

Thus the Central Government and State Governments have taken various steps for the promotion of tourism and attainment of the goal of sustainable tourism development.

SUSTAINABLLE TOURISM

The concept of sustainability means that mankind must live within the capacity of the environment that supports. Sustainable development has been defined briefly as "that which meets the needs of the present without compromising the ability of future generations to meet their own needs".

The definition brings out certain important aspects of sustainable tourism: -

➤ Conservation and enhancement of resources for the future generation

➤ Protection of biological diversity

➤ Equity within and between generations

➤ Integration of environmental, social and economic considerations

The concept of sustainable development is all about conservation and stewardship of resources for the future. The support for ecologically sustainable development emerging strongly in the tourism sector, as it is the logical way of balancing environmental concerns with growth and development of the industry. Environmental problems facing the world today are of such magnitude that urgent actions have to be taken at the highest levels to counter this fatal degradation. But it is not just enough for government organisations to work towards sustainable development. Every individual, every neighborhood, and every community has to contribute in every away possible to get close to the goal. Since the earth summit, the concept of sustainable development has been placed firmly on the global agenda. This issue is assuming great significance in the development of tourism in India also.

Tourism activities depend upon nature and natural heritage, it is essential to ensure that tourism development is ecologically sustainable –ecological process must not be neglected. Similarly tourism offers real experience of unique culture of the country. Hence the development should ensure that social and cultural sustainable tourism development compatible with the culture and values of the local people.

The World Tourism Organization (WTO) defined sustainable tourism development as "that which meets the needs of present tourist and host regions while protecting and enhancing opportunities for the future. It is envisaged as leading to the management of all resources in such a way that economic, social and aesthetic needs can be fulfilled while maintaining cultural integrity, essential for ecological process, biological diversity and life supporting system".

Thus tourism has to be human and adapted to the needs of the tourist, respond to the needs of the local communities, be socio-economic and culturally well planned and environmentally sound. The tourism must offer products that are operated in harmony with the local environment, community attitudes and culture so that they become permanent beneficiaries and not the victims of tourism. The basic cultural identity of these local people should not be adversely affected. Sustainability also ensures economically sustainable-development process in the efficient management of resources and such management to ensure that the resource supports the future as well as the present generation.

Thus sustainable tourism aims to: -

➢ Improve the quality of life of people.

➢ Provide good experience to the tourists.

➢ Maintain the quality of environment that is essential for both tourists and the local community.

Tourism can be one of the effective tools for building a prosperous community economically, socially and culturally. It must be environmentally sustainable and based on the sustenance of the natural and cultural base.

Each destination should examine whether it has adequate attractions and facilities for tourism and there is a potential for tourism generating markets to be open to exploitation.

The carrying capacity is the central principle in environmental protection and sustainable tourism development. It determines the maximum use of any place without causing negative effects on resources on community, economy and culture.

Thus tourism has to be environmentally sustainable in both natural and cultural environment Basic Guidelines for achieving sustainable tourism. The following are certain guidelines that have to be followed to achieve

Sustainable tourism:

➢ A general tourism policy incorporating sustainable tourism objectives at national regional and local level should be followed.

➢ Targets established for the planning, development and operation of tourism involving various government departments, public and private sector companies, community groups and experts could provide widest possible safeguards for success.

➢ Primary consideration should be given to the protection of natural and cultural assets.

➢ All tourism participants will follow ethical and sound behavioral and conservative rules regarding nature, culture, economy, and community value system.

➢ The distribution of tourism development project should be rationed on the basis of equity.

➢ Public awareness of benefits tourism and how to mitigate its negative impacts should be pursued.

➢ Local people would be encouraged to assume leadership roles in planning and development.

In the Tourism Policy, 1982 the guidelines in Eco-tourism have attempted to achieve sustainability in tourism. It indicates that the key players in the ecotourism are Central Government and state governments, local authorities, developers, operators, visitors and local community. Each of them has to be sensitive to the environment and local traditions and follow the guidelines for successfully development of sustainable tourism.

Ecotourism

Ecotourism, also known as ecological tourism, is responsible travel to fragile, pristine, and usually protected areas that strives to be low-impact and (often) small-scale. It helps educate the traveler; provides funds for conservation; directly benefits the economic development and political empowerment of local communities; and fosters respect for different cultures and for human rights.Take only memories and leave only footprints is a very common slogan in protected areas. Tourist destinations are shifting to low carbon emissions following the trend of visitors more focused in being environmentally responsible adopting a sustainable behavior.

Recession tourism

Recession tourism is a travel trend, which evolved by way of the world economic crisis. Identified by American entrepreneur Matt Landau(2007), recession tourism is defined by low-cost, high-value experiences taking place of once-popular generic retreats. Various recession tourism hotspots have seen business boom during the recession thanks to comparatively low costs of living and a slow world job market suggesting travelers are elongating trips where their money travels further.

Social tourism

Social tourism is the extension of the benefits of tourism to disadvantaged people who otherwise could not afford to travel for their education of recreation. It includes youth hostels and low-priced holiday accommodation run by church and voluntary organisations, trade unions, or in Communist times publicly owned enterprises. In May 1959, at the second Congress of Social Tourism in Austria, Walter Hunziker proposed the following definition: "Social tourism is a type of tourism practiced by low income groups, and which is rendered possible and facilitated by entirely separate and therefore easily recognizable services".

CHAPTER – 3
TOURISM DEVELOPMENT

According to both the World Tourism Organization (WTO), and the World Travel Tourism Council (WTTC) the travel and tourism industry is the largest industry and employer in the world. Upon completion of your degree you will possess a sound theoretical understanding of the comprehensive study of tourism. This will include knowledge related to the growth and development of tourism throughout the world in historical, spatial and economic terms; the economic, ecological, and socio-cultural impacts of tourism in both the developing and developed world; and the system of tourism production, product development, service delivery, and consumption by diverse domestic and international market segments. Other areas of study include the psychological foundations of travel motivations, visitor perceptions, and their experiences at destinations, as well as host-guest interactions. The program encompasses local, regional and global perspectives in the study of tourism.

Through the required internship component of the degree program, students will gain practical experiences for professional positions in various travel, tourism, and related fields. Exposure to the businesses of heritage tourism, sustainable tourism, resort management, and meeting and convention planning will prepare you for a successful career in the fast-growing travel and tourism industry.

Trend of Tourism Development

The important trends of tourism in the world are as follow:

Increasing Choices of Destinations

For several decades, Western Europe has been a popular destination for international tourists. However, as tourists have got used to visiting Western Europe, they become curious about the less explored parts of the world such as Eastern Europe, the Asia-Pacific area and the less developed parts of the world including Africa. In general, there appears to be a slow shift of tourist arrivals from the economic advanced countries to the less developed ones.

Mercurial Responses to Changing Economic Environment

The potential for tourism growth is enormous throughout the world. As the production of goods and services increases, people have more disposable income and more leisure time. At the same time, a better-educated population would like to travel for different purposes such as recreation, education and health. Although there may be economic setbacks that will discourage tourism development, tourism has always found new ways to flourish. For example, many people would rather change their travel destinations or spending patterns than give up their vacation. Also, there are tour packages to suit every taste and income level.

Governments Encouraging Tourism Development

As many countries recognize the potential contribution of tourism to their economy, there will be increasing competition in the development and promotion of tourism among countries in future.

Sustainable Forms of Tourism

In future, tourism development will no longer be determined solely by economic consideration. It is suggested that tourism development should not abuse the natural environment.

As environmental issues are becoming a worldwide concern, there will be new forms of tourism such as "eco-tourism", "agri-tourism" and "green tourism".

"Special-Interest Tourism" Changes Forms of Tourism

Due to cultural and social changes, there have been significant changes in the pattern of international tourism. "Special-interest tourism" (such as weight-losing and mind-broadening) has been developed to cater for the wide range of interests of tourists.

Increasing Ability to Travel of Young People and the Elderly

It is suggested that in the next decade, the number of tourists of the following two age groups will increase faster than that of the others: senior citizens and young people. Due to changes in socio-economic conditions such as better retirement benefits, more senior citizens can afford to travel after retirement. Moreover, better education and new travel opportunities enable young people to travel more.

Information Technology Contributing to Tourism Development

Information technology will become all-powerful in influencing destination choice and distribution. Travel suppliers and promoters are using information technology to identify and communicate with travellers through promotion and information supply, and to assist the travellers in their choice of destinations. Travellers that are familiar with surfing on the Internet for information and reservations could make their travel arrangements by themselves. As a result, the traditional distribution channels of delivery through intermediaries are being affected.

Service of Intermediaries Professional and Personalized

The role of travel agents is now changing from that of intermediaries to that of a provider of personal service and professional expertise.

Theme Based Tourism Product Diversification

Theme based tourism product is being developed with a combination of the three Es – entertainment, excitement and education.

Terrorist Attack Enhanced Concern of Travel Safety

Air traffic control systems play a major role in overall air travel safety such as collision avoidance, precision landing aids and ground obstacle avoidance.

Air security issues such as security screening at airports, permanent reinforcement of cockpit doors, public safety are also being major concerns especially after the September 11 Terrorist Attack in New York and Washington

TOURISM DEVELOPMENT IN INDIA

Tourism development in India has passed through many phases. At Government level the development of tourist facilities was taken up in a planned manner in 1956 coinciding with the Second Five Year Plan. The approach has evolved from isolated planning of single unit facilities in the Second and Third Five Year Plans. The Sixth Plan marked the beginning of a new era when tourism began to be considered a major instrument for social integration and economic development. But it was only after the 80's that tourism activity gained momentum. The Government took several significant steps. A National Policy on tourism was announced in 1982.

Later in 1988, the National Committee on Tourism formulated a comprehensive plan for achieving a sustainable growth in tourism. In 1992, a National Action Plan was prepared and in 1996 the National Strategy for Promotion of Tourism was drafted. In 1997, a draft new tourism policy in tune with the economic policies of the Government and the trends in tourism development was published for public debate. The draft policy is now under revision. The proposed policy recognises the roles of

Central and State governments, public sector undertakings and the private sector in the development of tourism. The need for involvement of Panchayati Raj institutions, local bodies, non-governmental organisations and the local youth in the creation of tourism facilities has also been recognised.

The other major development that took place were the setting up of the India Tourism Development Corporation in 1966 to promote India as a tourist destination and the Tourism Finance Corporation in 1989 to finance tourism projects. Altogether, 21 Government-run Hotel Management and Catering Technology Institutes and 14 Food Craft Institutes were also established for imparting specialised training in hoteliering and catering.

Tourist Attractions

India is a country known for its lavish treatment to all visitors, no matter where they come from. Its visitor-friendly traditions, varied life styles and cultural heritage and colourful fairs and festivals held abiding attractions for the tourists.

The other attractions include beautiful beaches, forests and wild life and landscapes for eco-tourism, snow, river and mountain peaks for adventure tourism, technological parks and science museums for science tourism; centres of pilgrimage for spiritual tourism; heritage trains and hotels for heritage tourism. Yoga, ayurveda and natural health resorts also attract tourists. The Indian handicrafts particularly, jewellery, carpets, leather goods, ivory and brass work are the main shopping items of foreign tourists. The estimates available through surveys indicate that nearly forty per cent of the tourist expenditure on shopping is spent on such items.

Growth

Domestic tourism is as old as the Indian society. According to available statistics, domestic tourism has grown substantially during the last one decade. It increased to 167 million in 1998 from just 64 million in 1990, thus registering a compound annual growth of 12.8 per cent.

The growth of inbound tourism since Independence has been quite impressive. It was just around 17 thousand in 1951. From this level it rose to 2.36 million in 1998. Tourism receipts on the other hand have grown at a phenomenal rate of 17 per cent to Rs.11,540 crore in 1998 from Rs.7.7 crore in 1951.

Economic Impact

Tourism has emerged as an instrument of employment generation, poverty alleviation and sustainable human development. During 1998-99, employment generation through tourism was estimated at 14.79 million. Foreign exchange earnings from the tourism sector during 1998-99 were estimated at Rs.12,011 crore. Tourism has thus become the second largest net foreign exchange earner for the country. Tourism also contributed Rs.24,241 crore during 1998-99 towards the country's Gross Domestic Product (GDP).

Thrust Areas

In order to speed up the development of tourism in the

country several thrust areas have been identified for accomplishment during the Ninth Five Year Plan (1997-2002). The important ones are development of infrastructure, products, trekking, winter sports, wildlife and beach resorts and streamlining of facilitation procedures at airports, human resource development and facilitating private sector participation in the growth of infrastructure.

Organisation

The organisations involved in the development of tourism in India are the Ministry of Tourism with its 21 field offices within the country and 18 abroad, Indian Institute of Tourism and Travel Management, National Council for Hotel Management and Catering Technology, India Tourism Development Corporation, Indian Institute of Skiing and Mountaineering and the National Institute of Water Sports.

Boosting Tourism

Some of the recent initiatives taken by the Government to boost tourism include grant of export house status to the tourism sector and incentives for promoting private investment in the form of Income Tax exemptions, interest subsidy and reduced import duty. The hotel and tourism-related industry has been declared a high priority industry for foreign investment which entails automatic approval of direct investment up to 51 per cent of foreign equity and allowing 100 per cent non-resident Indian investment and simplifying rules regarding the grant of approval to travel agents, tour operators and tourist transport operators.

Celebrations

During the Golden Jubilee celebrations of India as a Republic, the Ministry of Tourism made special efforts to publicise the tourism potential of India. The first-ever Indian Tourism Day was celebrated on January 25, 1998. Bauddha Mahotsav was organised from 24th October to 8th November 1998. The Year 1999 was celebrated as Explore India Millennium Year by presenting a spectacular tableau on the cultural heritage of India at the Republic Day Parade and organising India Tourism Expo in New Delhi and Khajuraho.

The Wong La Millennium was held from April 1999 to January 2001. A special calendar of events has been formulated for highlighting contributions to Millennium events by various places in all the States. An official website of the Ministry of Tourism has also been created for facilitating dissemination of information on tourism.

Constraints

The major constraint in the expansion of international tourist traffic to India is non-availability of adequate infrastructure including adequate air seat capacity, accessibility to tourist destinations, accommodation and trained manpower in sufficient number.

Poor visitor experience, particularly, due to inadequate infrastructural facilities, poor hygienic conditions and incidents of touting and harassment of tourists in some places are factors that contribute to poor visitor experience. To sum up, Indian tourism has vast potential for generating employment and earning large sums of foreign exchange besides giving a fillip to the country's overall economic and social development. Much has been achieved by way of increasing air seat capacity, increasing trains and railway connectivity to important tourist destinations, four-laning of roads connecting important tourist centres and increasing availability of accommodation by adding heritage hotels to the hotel industry and encouraging paying guest accommodation. But much more remains to be done.

Since tourism is a multi-dimensional activity, and basically a service industry, it would be necessary that all wings of the Central and State governments, private sector and voluntary organisations become active partners in the endeavour to attain sustainable growth in tourism if India is to become a world player in the tourist industry.

Tourism concepts and principles -Tourism and the tourist

The Meaning of "Travel", "Tourism" and "Tourist"

Concepts of 'Travel' and 'Tourism' Travel

Travel comprises all journeys from one place to another. It includes all journeys made by people who enter a country for leisure, to work, reside, study or who just pass through a country without stopping.

Tourism

(a) Tourism means the temporary short-term movement of

people to destinations outside the places where they normally live and work, as well as their activities during their stay at these destinations. (All tourism should have some travel, but not all travel is tourism.)

(b) Tourism comprises the activities of persons travelling to and staying in places outside their usual environment for less than a year and whose main purpose of travel is other than the exercise of an activity remunerated from within the place visited. The term "usual environment" is intended to exclude trips within the area of usual residence and frequent and regular trips between the domicile and the workplace and other community trips of a routine character.

The Meaning of "Travel", "Tourism" and "Tourist"
Meaning
Travel

Travel comprises all journeys from one place to another. It includes all journeys made by people who enter a country for leisure, to work, reside, study or who just pass through a country without stopping.

Tourism

(a) Tourism means the temporary short-term movement of people to destinations outside the places where they normally live and work, as well as their activities during their stay at these destinations. (All tourism should have some travel, but not all travel is tourism.)

(b) Tourism comprises the activities of persons travelling to and staying in places outside their usual environment for less than a year and whose main purpose of travel is other than the exercise of an activity remunerated from within the place visited. The term "usual environment" is intended to exclude trips within the area of usual residence and frequent and regular trips between the domicile and the workplace and other community trips of a routine character.

Concept of Tourism

Tourism is the world's number one industry, and the chances are that you come across quite a few tourists, particularly in the summer months, but perhaps year round, depending on where you live. The terms tourism and tourists are words that we are familiar with, but what do they actually mean to people who work in the industry. Let's have a look at what to us is probably a pair of typical tourists: The Wongs are an Hong Kong couple who are in Malaysia on a two-week tour. They've spent some time in Sabah and now they're in Malacca, touring around and seeing the historical sights and beaches.They like to stay in comfortable hotels and while in Malacca they spent a couple of nights at the beach resort hotel. They bought a number of gifts to take back home – mostly Malacca's crafts. They visited the different historical sites in Malacca and they've taken lots of photographs to show their friends and family when they get back home. In a couple of days they will travel to Kuala Lumpur to catch their return flight home to Hong Kong.

Introduction to Tourism Government

Why Governments are involved in Tourism? Governments are involved in tourism for a variety of reasons.

➤ Tourism has an impact on the economy of a country (it brings in foreign currency, impacts on the balance of payments, increases employment and aids regional development).

➤ Tourism involves movement across national frontiers - governments have to control and monitor this.

➤ Tourism is often used to enhance national image – governments are keen to ensure that foreigners have a positive perception of their country.

➤ The tourism product may need protection as well as development through government aid. Many core tourist attractions are public property (landscapes, natural and built heritage)

➤ Government provides or has an interest in the infrastructure upon which tourism exists - public services, roads, railways, airports, ferry terminals etc., although it should be remembered that very little infrastructures are provided solely for tourism

Tourism concepts and principles – The tourism industry

The part played by government in the development and management of tourism Government The industry is very diverse and government involvement is necessary to regulate and co-ordinate activities and provide consumer protection

➢ To provide finance necessary for marketing and development at the destination

➢ Taxation - many governments use tourism as a source of tax revenue. In Hong Kong, we are taxed on accommodation and air travel.

Role of Government in the Development of Tourism
The Major Roles of Government in the Development of Tourism

1. Planning and facilitating tourism

2. Control and supervision of tourism

➢ Refusal or granting of permission in planning

➢ Control of the export currency

➢ Supervision of tourism industry

3. Direct ownership of components of the tourism industry

4. Promoting tourism to domestic home and overseas markets

➢ Active involvement

➢ Investment support

➢ Operational support

➢ Research and planning

CHAPTER – 4
INTERNATIONAL TOURISM IN INDIA:
INTRODUCTION

India initiated economic reforms as an aftermath of a serious foreign exchange crisis. The number and the pace of reforms have been increasing ever since. The scope of external liberalization has increased many-fold in several fields, with difficult withdrawl conditions under WTO agreements. Despite all these efforts, the Balance of Trade continues to be adverse, and so is the case with balance in the current account, if the private transfers were not supporting the same. Even then the Balance of Payment position can not be said to be satisfactory, if one takes into account the transfers in capital account and the external debt position, the latter having crossed U.S. $ 100 billion mark in the year 2002. The next round of negotiations at WTO is due soon, in which GATS, including Tourism, is likely to be an important item. International Tourism is a U.S. $ 4 trillion plus service sector, growing at an average rate of 10% per year. The importance of it for India can be realised from the fact that a 2.5% share in even one year can wipe off India's total external debt and an increase by 0.25% share can more than off set the adverse balance of trade, and ease foreign exchange pressure on the economy.

If India wishes to negotiate and open Tourism sector further to benefit from the international tourism business, it has to think strategically and gear up internally to develop appropriate physical, human resource, and other organisational infrastructure in an integrated manner, which can meet the varied needs of international tourists. Failing this, if the tourism sector is opened further for the external players, India may become only a minor tool in the value creation process in the international tourism business in India. It must prepare for playing the role of the main player, who not only helps in enhancing the value creation, but also captures and controls the value created. The major benefits otherwise would be captured by other international players.

The papers points towards several strategic inadequacies, gaps and vulnerabilities that are typically observed in the process of management of tourism in the country, which need to be attended to. The paper also indicates the need for strong, scholarly, analytical support required for the purpose, which can be extended by the academicians in the country.

STRATEGIC GAPS AND VULNERABILITIES
1. INTRODUCTION

India initiated economic reforms as an aftermath of a serious foreign exchange crisis. The number and the pace of reforms have been increasing ever since. The scope of external liberalization has increased many-fold in several fields, with difficult with drawl conditions under WTO agreements. Despite all these efforts, the Balance of Trade continues to be adverse, and so is the case with balance in the current account, if the private transfers were not supporting the same. Even then the Balance of Payment position can not be said to be satisfactory, if one takes into account the transfers in capital account and the external debt position, the latter having crossed U.S. $ 100 billion mark in the year 2002.

The next round of negotiations at WTO is due soon, in which GATS, including Tourism, is likely to be an important item. International Tourism is a U.S. $ 4 trillion plus service sector, growing at an average rate of 10% per year. The importance of it for India can be realised from the fact that a 2.5% share in even one year can wipe off India's total external debt and an increase by 0.25% share can more than off set the adverse balance of trade, and ease foreign exchange pressure on the economy.

If India wishes to negotiate and open Tourism sector further to benefit from the international tourism business, it has to think strategically and gear up internally to develop appropriate physical, human resource, and other organisational infrastructure in an integrated manner, which can meet the varied needs of international tourists. Failing this, if the tourism sector is opened further for the external players, India may become only a minor tool in the value creation process in the international tourism business in India.

It must prepare for playing the role of the main player, who not only helps in enhancing the value creation, but also captures and controls the value created. The major benefits otherwise would be captured by other international players.

To understand the strategic gaps and vulnerability, it is necessary to revisit three basic concepts, the concepts of (tourism) business, strategic management and value creation, value capture and value control in the (tourism) business.

2. CONCEPT OF TOURISM BUSINESS

What is tourism? Oxford dictionary defines tourism as the commercial organisation and operation of holidays and visits to places of interest. Tourist is a person who travels for pleasure. The word Tourist does not encompass all kinds of persons who are on tour. The meaning of the word tour includes:

(a) A journey for pleasure in which several different places are covered.

(b) A short trip to view or inspect something.

The word tourism and tourist relate only to part (a) and not (b). This distinction is important to bear in mind because although some of the needs of the two are apparently common, like stay and travel arrangements, they are qualitatively different. Furthermore, some of the needs of (a) are not common with those of (b) mentioned above. Mixing the two conceptually, leads to creating an infrastructure, which serves some of the need of both, but ignores many of needs of tourist. Gradually the pressure of capacity utilization leads to focus on the latter and in operational terms the very concept of business changes from tourism to hospitality, transport etc.

3. THE VALUE CHAIN ACTIVITES OF TOURISM BUSINESS

Developing from the concept of tourist, in physical terms, the gamut of activities relatingto international tourism business can be charted out as below.

➢ Language (destination)

➢ Currency

➢ Level of Familiarity

At each of the nodal points, the international tourist may require arrangements for stay, food and travel. These are common to the people who are on business/official tours also, but with several differences, the expenses in the latter case are not to be borne by the person himself (office bears it) unlike the case of tourist. It is also not done as per entitlement. Tourist has to optimise his expenses. Further, there is a marked difference in the level of familiarity with the place of visit (especially on the subsequent visits) and the responsibility for making various arrangement lies with office, not with the person himself.

The distinction does not end there. Tourist is not going to complete a job. His visits are determined by the attractiveness of the place. Attractiveness of the place could be natural phenomenon (like Niagara Falls) or manmade on like Eiffel Tower or Disney Land.

Needless to add, tourists do not go to destination to gain theoretical or visual knowledge of it; which they can do even by being at their place, thanks to technological development in the present internet era. They come to experience it, personally, in the total setting. In this context the arrangements of foods, stay (and travel) too can add to attractiveness, if they are unique, tasty (comfortable) and hygienic (safe and affordable).

It may be noted that as the distance between the place of origin and the destination (place of interest) increases, tourist tends to visit larger number of sites/spend larger number of day to maximise satisfaction from the amount of money and time spent. It is rare for an international tourist to come and see just one place, spending thousands of rupees (equivalent) and several days in travel. He then starts seeking package of places of interest.

Packages are sought not only in terms of sites, but also services (stay, food and travel etc.), cities/ states and groups of people to enhance pleasure together and guard against lack of familiarity.There are other needs too, which are not easily realised such as availability of necessary amount of money as and where required.

The tourist needs to know the details of the site, its attractiveness as well definitiveness and the ease of making arrangements for travel, stay and food. Over and above this, the requirements of certainty, reliability and prompt information about disturbance causing events also assume significance for him. An additional demand arises on account of differences in languages. The above does not purport to be a comprehensive and exhaustive, but only an indicative list of all the needs of tourists emanating from different origins and conveys the variation in the nature and magnitude of requires as the distance between place of origin and destination increases. These need to be elaborated and prioritized through research studies.

The significance of the above discussion lies in the fact that these requirements of the tourists get determined by the definition of target in terms of place of origin and the demographic variables of tourists. The requirements of tourist from Kenya would be different from those of Sweden, the requirements of senior citizens as tourists would be different from the adolescents. The preparation required to be made for attracting tourists and catering to their needs at the destination may go haywire, if the customer requirements are not properly defined before hand.

The uniqueness of tourism business lies in the fact that it is not a single service, but involves a large variety of different, exclusive and specialized services, which can be provided by different group catering to hospitality, transport and travel, unique, attractive site etc.

There is thus, an additional task or business: that of integration of these services. For example, the tourist would like to know about the places he may like visit, and as he goes to decide it, he wants whether accommodation and travel reservation within his budget are possible and if so, could he have them confirmed.

Any loose link in the entire value chain of services needed by him, may jeopardize his plan and pleasure. He is willing to pay the price for the role of integrator is ensuring certainty and reliability. The success of tourism business perhaps depends as much, if not more, on this integration aspect, as the quality and variety of the specialized saves of transport, accommodation etc.

4. THE VALUE CREATION, CAPTURE AND CONTROL IN TOURISM BUSINESS

The value chain of tourism business starts from the activity of identifying the customer, presenting them the attractiveness of destination in an interactive manner, helping him in travel, accommodation & other reservations, helping in money transfer etc, and actually taking to and entertaining him at the destination site, besides taking care at nodal, transit points. The total money spent by a tourist is the total value created in the tourism business.

Income from impulse purchases like specialities, memoirs etc. and all other money spent by him on account of his "pleasure travel" constitute the total value2 added in the tourism business. The sharing or capture of the total value created by different service providers depends not only upon the absolute quality of service provided by individual supplier, but their ability to control it. It is much the same way as in the case of computer hardware sales. Out of a total price of a PC say Rs. 40,000, half of it is captured by the supplier of processors and mother board etc. With every effort to assemble and sell a PC, the sale of processor is assured. Though a high amount of efforts are required to assemble and sell PCs, the major value is captured by processor supplier and it can strategically control the entire sales.

The same may turnout to be the case of Tourism also if due care is not taken to develop adequate safeguards measures when the sector is opened for the foreign players. Further discussion on the issue is deferred to a later section.

5. STRATEGIC MANAGEMENT

The concept of strategic management can help in analysis of strategic gaps with reference to management of International Tourism in India. Strategic Management can be understood by looking at the types of managerial decisions. Ansoff3 has classified the organisational decisions into three broad categories; namely, the strategic, the administrative and the operating decisions. The strategic decisions (covered under strategy formulation) are concerned with the issue of setting the direction in which the organisation will move or the course that the organisation would follow in the future. These cover the decisions regarding the organisation's mission, objectives and the strategies (i.e., the product/ market scope). The administrative decisions (commonly referred to as strategy implementation), on the other and relate to the task of gearing, up the existing set-up i.e., physical, human and organisational infrastructure to meet the requirement of business/operations in the future. Typically they cover such issues as the resource allocation, changes in the organizational structure, systems, skills technology, organisation culture and key functional policies. Taken together they cover the entire scope of strategic management function. Finally, there are operating decisions concerning various transactions or the actual operations.

Strategic management deals with decisions that fall in the strategic and administrative decision categories mentioned above. Strategic management may be defined as a stream of decisions and actions which lead to the development of effective strategy or strategies to help achieve corporate objectives. Strategic management may thus be called as a process by which the top management determines the long term direction and performance of organisation, by ensuring that careful formulation, proper implementation and continuous evaluation of strategy takes place.

It is necessary here to explain the concept of corporate strategy. Corporate strategy can be defined as "a statement of organisation mission, objectives, strategy, policies and major plans and programmes of actions, described in a way that conveys what business we are in and why are we in this business".

This definition brings out the need for organizational clarity about the mission, objectives and strategies, to integrate or unify the organizational efforts. Corporate strategy may, thus, be understood as the outcome of strategic formulation process.

6. THE STRATEGIC GAPS

Gaps in the Concept of Business

As mentioned earlier, the strategic management forces the management to be clear on what business an organisation is in. Strategic management concerns with two significant discussions related to a future of an organisation.

These are:

(i) What business the organisation would be in the future (in terms of produces market scope) and why?

(ii) How it proposes to gear up to meet the requirements of physical infrastructures, human resources (skills, style etc.) and organisational resources (structures, systems, shared values etc.) of the future business?

As elaborated in an earlier section, the value system of tourism industry tends to encompasses all the services required from the place of origin of the international tourist to the destination. The total gamut of services that need to be provided can be broadly classified into two categories.

A. Promotional and developmental (to induce, attract bring tourists from his place of origin to the state of destination).

B. To cater to his requirements once they reach the place, to help them gain memorable experience of the visit.

1. Knowledge of

* Tourist places and their attractiveness

* Availability of proper

- Accommodation

- Transport/Carrier

- Food

- Accessories

* Money Transfer facilities

* Booking/Reservation

2. Assurance of the

* The above arrangement

* Safety /security

3. Helps and guidance in case of exigencies

a). Actually providing on their arrival at different places, the facilities of

- Accommodation

- Food

- Transport

- Communication

- Money Exchange facility

b). Providing facilities for site seeing/ shopping etc. as promised

c). Providing timely guidance for any change in programme needed on account of emergency/ exigencies

d). Assistance of interpretation to overcome problems arising on account of difficulties language barriers

The first major strategic gap that is stunning one, is observed in the concept of business itself. At present, the country seems to be geared only for entertaining the international tourists on their arrival, focusing on activities related to "B" part mentioned above, rather than focusing equally on inducing and attracting international tourist to India. A visit to tourist developments corporations will reveal the glaring nature of this gap.

An international tourist can not know and get the services relating to "A" part from the place of his origin. The websites of different tourist corporation are not integrated even for information, leave alone providing other services, like booking/reservation of accommodation, air/rail ticketing etc. Each website seems to be quite independent of other and does not provide information in an integrated, building block manner.

Customer Segmentation Gaps

The international tourists are taken as a homogeneous group. The word "international" is thus used loosely rather than identifying and focussing on different geographic and demographic segments to develop appropriate infrastructure to uniquely meet the requirements of different tourists segments. This is exemplified by the publicity material that is available in English Hindi or other vernacular language which can not meet the requirements of a nature German, Swiss, French, Italian, Spanish Swede, Dutch or other European tourists.

One may be surprised to learn that the hotels, reservation and such other agencies may not even know from where is the potential market, USA, Europe, Japan, Kenya or Singapore. A knowledge of the fact that the biggest chunk in the international tourism is constituted by European tourists, may considerably help in sharpening and focusing strategy. Efforts are made to design Buddha Circuit, Taj Circuit etc.

But these may not be items of common/ equal level of interest to international tourist from Japan and Eurpoe. Same is the case of lack of understanding about their demographic patterns. For example, there seems to be no cognition of the fact that there are different segments by age group and that the requirements of each age group is different.

Lack of Clarity on Objectives

The individual services providers like hotels, airlines etc. cater to tourist alright, but they can not be sure of attracting them because all by themselves they can not determine it. The tourism development corporations were expected to do the job. But a typical list of objectives would indicate that they had various activities listed to entertain the tourist ones they come to country. There is no mention that they wish to earn foreign exchange and bring more tourists from different parts of the globe.

They thus reduce themselves to play the role of individual service provider, concerned primary with increase in their capacity utilisation through variety of customers, rather than gearing up to bring the international tourists here.

Gap in Integration

The essence of strategic management is not only futuristic but also ensuring integration ensuring that the requirement of infrastructures and operations for international tourism in India are properly taken care of. Presently there seem to be lot of gaps in the interlinkages between various services. The hospitality industry (hotels etc.) treat tourism more as an as add on activity. The local site seeing is some what better connected in physical terms, but there is little standardisation and assurance of quality of service. The international money transfer facility is not provided by any domestic agency. The list of certified hotels and guest houses is not available to the tourists except though foreign travel agencies.

There is little or no inter- connectivity across various service providers and across the states. The international tourist has to decide various arrangements before commencement of journey. But at present an international tourist may not even know about tourist facilities available at different sites, directly from any domestic, Indian travel agent and other players. He has to reach the country before he decides finer details.There is no integrated system to system to let international tourist get successive levels of information. There is no single agency to take care of missing links and ensure integration of various services as a cohesive whole, rather than presenting services in a fragmented manner.

The task of ensuring appropriate integration is not so difficult in the present internet era, But major players who can effectively play the role of integrator such as State Bank of India , Bank of Baroda, etc. who have large network of branches both in India and abroad and also have close interact businesses, are feeling shy of entering the tourism business and playing critical integrative role and really make tourism a money spinning and foreign exchange earner.

7. Objectives of State Tourism Development Corporation

1. To promote, take over, develop, start, purchase, construct, take on lease, maintain, manage and operate hotels, restaurants, motels, travellers' lodges, guest houses and other places for the purpose of boarding, lodging and stay of the tourists; canteens, cafeteria, places of tourist interest like wild life sanctuaries, beauty .and recreational places like parks, avenues and galleries, handicrafts emporia, establishments, undertaking enterprises and such other activities of any description with a view to develop, facilitate and promote tourism in the stat.

2. To enter into any arrangement for taking over any or all of the assets and liabilities of any department of the state government or of the Government of India connected with the development of tourism and in particular as a going concern all or any of the Tourists' Homes/State government Guest Houses/ Travellers' bungalows and catering establishments already established and maintained by the state Government or by the Government of India in various places and to run the same with the object of promoting tourism.

3. To establish and manage transport units, travel and transport counters, import, purchase, lease and run or otherwise operate buses, coaches, trucks, launches, ropeways, aircraft, helicopters,

inland, waterways and other modes of transport and to act as travel agents I for airlines, railways, shipping companies etc.

4. To produce, distribute and sell tourist publicity materials; edit, design, print, publish, sell or otherwise deal with books magazines, periodicals, folders, guide books, pamphlets, bills, posters, picture post cards, diaries, calendars, slides, cinematograph films and other materials for the purpose of giving publicity to and developing tourism.

5. To provide, arrange or conduct entertainment for tourists by way of cultural shows, dances, music concerts, cabarets, ballets, film shows, sports and games, son-et-lumiere spectacles and others.

6. To provide or arrange shopping facilities for tourists, establish or manage shops including duty free shops, emporia and other places for selling travel requisites and other articles of tourist interest.

7. To carry on the business of restaurant keepers, wine and spirit merchants, licensed victualers, theatrical agents, box office keepers, concert room proprietors, hotel keepers, dramatic and musical publishers and printers and any other business, which can be carried on in connection with any of those objects as may seem calculated to render profitable any of the company's property and rights for the time being.

8. To establish art galleries for the exhibition of paintings, engravings, sculptures, jewelry and other works of art and to buy, sell and deal in works of art of all kinds.

9. To acquire land and construct, develop and maintain wayside amenities and picnic spots.

10. To organise or conduct all inclusive tours by roads, rail, sea, air or otherwise and to enter into agreements for this purpose.

8. STRATEGIC VULNERABILITY

The fact that tourism world wide is a U.S.$ 4 trillion business, opens up great opportunity for India to benefit from it in terms of earning foreign exchange and mitigate adverse balance of trade account. An increase of 0.25% share in the international tourism business can overcome the pressure of earning foreign exchange that has to be arranged through high interest bearing bonds and deposits, which add to self perpetuating crisis.

The potential business may be lost if India does not gear up to bridge the strategic gaps mentioned above. Worse still these potential may be exploited to the hill by the foreign players by bridging the gaps. Despite huge international tourism business in India, the country may not benefit in terms of getting foreign exchange as the same may be appropriated by them. The booking of international travel may be done by foreign carriers and exchange and commission associated with transfer of money may be appropriated by the international players like American Express, Thomas Cook etc, using Indian labour only. Even the booking of hotels may be done in foreign country and the foreign exchange may not flow to India.

A big chunk of total value created in the tourism business in the form of travel, accommodated money transfer, even shopping may be captured by the strong armed multinational player with world wide network and Indian service providers reduced to play only second fiddle.

Some recent studies show that the country has not gained benefits as expected by opening of Indian economy in terms of reducing international trade gap, technological capability building and globalisation1or enhanced global competitiveness and ability to earn foreign exchange on its own. The same may happen in the tourism sector if it opened without necessary ground work.

9. ACTION STRATEGIES

International tourism is an extremely tempting proposition in terms of potential of business especially foreign exchange earnings, for opening of tourism sector in the next round of negotiations. It may, however, turnout to be a mirage if the sector is opened without adequate preparation to gear up the strategic gaps. India currently is not geared to reap the advantage of first movers. Hence must avoid straight jacket opening.

It has to fine tune this gearing up with speed of opening tourism sector as per the provisions of negotiations at WTO. It has to carefully examine when and how much to open through (almost irreversible) specific commitments and what should be limitations put into effect to achieve this fine tuning.

The preparations for exploitation of international tourism business require as much attention of the government and industry as of the academicians. The governments need to play the first level integrator role in terms of setting priorities and expectations from the international tourism business. It has to play the role of promoters, persuading different providers (to bridge the gaps), who have not come forward to play the role like the banks. The industry has to develop mechanisms to ensure strong linkages among various service providers to make it an integrated whole, rather than behaving like a large number disjointed service providers. The academicians have to provide strong analytical support through research studies for identification of missing links in providing various services, pointing conceptual confusion in mission, objectives and strategies. In a nutshell the international tourism business has to be considered in its entirety by the three major contributors.

10. ISSUES FOR FUTURE RESEARCH

The paper highlights the need for several types of in-depth studies required to gear up for benefiting from the growing international tourism business. There is a need for study of international tourists needs (especially those related to the promotional and developmental aspects explained in section 3 of the paper) coming from different geographical areas. There is also a need for studying the appropriateness of existing infrastructure in light of the needs identified to understand the degree to which the present infrastructure is adequate or inadequate.

Only the in-depth studies can show whether there is need to focus more on utilisation of infrastructure already created rather than creating new ones. The country has paid huge price in the race for creating huge assets in the nineties in various sectors of industry leading to excessive infrastructure created. The mistake does not need to be repeated once again in this sector. There is also a need for validating the strategic gaps identified in the concept of business.

This will help in identifying to what extent the thrust of tourism strategy in India has been a lopsided one; focusing mainly on entertaining the international tourists who have come to India vs. bringing them to India and its different states. Studies are also required to ascertain the nature and level of efforts and investment required for bringing the international tourists to India. Further studies are also required to clarify the strategic focus of tourism industry; how much domestic and how much international tourism and why? Studies are also required to clarify the assumption of considering all the international tourists as a homogeneous group. Are there demographic segments that can help in designing the infrastructure in a better manner to meet specific and varied requirements of different segments? There is yet another set of studies required to identify the missing links in the tourism business at the country, state and city level that need to be taken care of? There is also a need for ascertaining whether tourism in general, and international tourism in particular, is being consider as an integrated business or an assortment of hospitality, entertainment and travel businesses by various players in the field. If so, what is the consequence of it in terms of loss of tourism business in general, and international tourism business in India, in particular. Last but not the least, there is a need for studies to understand how much of the value created in the international tourism in India is being captured and retained (especially the foreign currency part) in India and how much of it is captured and repatriated out of India by the international players. This is important as if due care is not taken then India may not benefit in terms of foreign exchange earning from this lucrative sector, what is a key consideration in negotiation at WTO for opening this sector.

CONCLUSION

International tourism is an extremely tempting proposition in terms of potential of business especially foreign exchange earnings, for opening of tourism sector in the next round of negotiations. If India wishes to negotiate and open Tourism sector further to benefit from the international tourism business, it has to think strategically and gear up internally to bridge the strategic gaps and develop appropriate physical, human resource, and other organisational infrastructure in an integrated manner, which can meet the varied needs of international tourists. Failing this, if the tourism sector is opened further for the external players, India may become only a minor tool in the value creation process in the international tourism business in India. It must prepare for playing the role of the main player, who not only helps in enhancing the value creation, but also captures and controls the value created. The major benefits otherwise would be captured by other international players.

REFERENCES

1. Denise Tollefson, **Nature and Society**, Geography 350, Fall 1999.

2. Michael E. Porter, **Competitive Advantage**, New York (1985) Free Press.

3. Ansoff, H.I., **Corporate Strategy**, New York (]965) McGraw Hill.

4. Rue, Les]ie, W., and Holland. Phyllos G., Strategic Management: Concepts and Experiences, Singapore (1989), McGraw Hill.

5. Andrews, K.R., **Concept of Corporate Strategy**, Homewood, Illinois (1972) Irwin.

6. http//:www.google.co.in

7. http//:www.wikipedia.com

www.ingramcontent.com/pod-product-compliance
Lightning Source LLC
Chambersburg PA
CBHW080833180526
45168CB00006B/2664